Things That Go

Anne Rockwell

A PUFFIN UNICORN

Unicorn is a registered trademark of E. P. Dutton.
Library of Congress number 86-6199
ISBN 0-14-054788-6

Published in the United States by
Dutton Children's Books,
a division of Penguin Books USA Inc.

Editor: Ann Durell   Designer: Edith T. Weinberg

Printed in Hong Kong by South China Printing Co.
First Unicorn Edition 1991
10 9 8 7

There are lots of things that go.
Turn the pages of this book and you will find
things that go...

Things That Go

tractor trailers

sports cars

sedans

motorcycles

station wagons

On The Road

convertibles

police cars

campers

tow trucks

tankers

Things That Go

water skis

motorboats

sailboats

canoes

rowboats

inner tubes

On The Water

sailboards

tugboats

fishing boats

surfboards

ocean liners

Things That Go

balloons

blimps

parachutes

satellites

kites

small planes

In The Air

big planes

helicopters

hang gliders

space shuttles

rockets

dogsleds

downhill skis

cross-country skis

ice skates

sleds

snowshoes

On Snow And Ice

sleighs

snowmobiles

bobsleds

snowblowers

snowplows

11

Things That Go

taxis

delivery bikes

motor scooters

garbage trucks

subways

In The City

fire engines

buses

hot-dog wagons

ambulances

vans

Things That Go

freight trains

pickup trucks

tractors

jeeps

utility trucks

In The Country

combines

hay wagons

school buses

lumber trucks

Things That Go

loaders

cement mixers

dump trucks

bulldozers

truck cranes

To Work

robots

sweepers

power shovels

lunch trucks

power rollers

hand trucks

Things That Go

carousels

baby carriages

bicycles

skateboards

strollers

In The Park

model sailboats

scooters

roller skates

tricycles

wheelchairs

ice-cream wagons

wagons

swings

wheelbarrows

cultivators

hose reels

croquet balls

In The Yard

lawn mowers

pogo sticks

garbage carts

rubber balls

toy fire engines

spreaders

toy trucks

vacuum cleaners

bathtub boats

toy trains

windup toys

TV trolleys

In The House

toy cars

doll carriages

baby walkers

kiddie cars

pull toys

push toys

hobbyhorses

I like things that go.